Unnatural Fauna:

A guide to the people of the American outdoors.

by Carol Poster

Illustrations by
John McMullen

ICS Books, Inc.
Merrillville, Indiana

Unnatural Fauna
Copyright © 1992 Carol Poster
10 9 8 7 6 5 4 3 2 1

Printed in U.S.A.

Published by:
ICS Books, Inc.
One Tower Plaza
107 E. 89th Avenue
Merrillville, IN 46410
800-541-7323

Library of Congress Cataloging-in-Publication Data

Poster, Carol.
    Unnatural fauna : a guide to the people of the American outdoors /
by Carol Poster ; illustrations by John McMullen.
        p.   cm.
    ISBN 0–934802–05-X : $7.99
    1. Outdoor recreation--Handbooks, manuals, etc.--Humor.
I. Title.
PN6231.096P67   1992   92-21090
818'.5402--dc20   CIP

Table of Contents

Introduction

Most of the field guides available do a good job of presenting information of very little significance to you. Which is more important—knowing whether a chipmunk or a golden mantled ground squirrel has been scarfing up spilled potato chips in the parking lot or knowing whether the guy whose ski tracks you are following is a local nordhead headed out to a secret powder stash or just some geek who got lost in the trees?

Just as the wildlife enthusiast needs to learn new ways of observing animals and a new vocabulary in order to understand the natural world, outdoors people need to learn similar tricks of observation and specialized lingo to understand the other people they meet in the outdoors.

Survival in the North American outdoors depends more on understanding people than on identifying animals. The human-grizzly conflicts in Glacier and Yellowstone National Parks are not caused by the unpredictable eating habits of the grizzly, but by the sloppy eating habits of people incapable of following the fairly simple camping precautions required in bear country.

This book will help you identify several human species commonly found in the outdoors—and avoid the worst of them.

On The Trails

Once upon a time, and a very long time ago, backcountry trails were the exclusive domain of hardy backpackers loaded down with hundreds of pounds of heavy duty gear. The advent of modern lightweight equipment has democratized hiking to the point where, on the average trail, you are as likely to encounter computer programmers on holiday wearing above-the-ankle polyester pants and Star Trek T-shirts as hardy Swiss mountaineers in knickers and rag wool socks.

This chapter lists some of the more common species you are likely to encounter on the trails of our National Parks and Forests.

DUDE/DUDETTE (Dudus gnarliest)

DUDE/DUDETTE (Dudus gnarliest)

Tracks: Gets significant air time on skateboard;
   only touches down rarely.

Appearance: Baggy shorts, oversized T-shirt
   advertising rock band.

Call: Little understood Southern California
   idiolect.

Where found: Favorite locales are rock concerts
   and beaches. Resigned to school and trips with
   parents. Breeds in Southern California,
   migrates widely.

Feeding Habits: Eats pineapple pizza and drinks
   imported beer.

Scat: Gum wrappers, torn lime green shoe laces.

EASTERN INTELLECTUAL (Academia urbanus)

Tracks: Hurachi sandals.

Appearance: Buys outdoor gear at L.L. Bean and
   Eddie Bauer and formal clothes at Banana Republic.

Call: "Kafkaesque".

Where found: Usually stays in college towns, but
   visits Mesa Verde in summer.

Feeding habits: Eats $10/lb. gorp, low fat fruit
   yogurt, and imported cheeses.

Scat: Fountain pens, books of experimental fiction.

EXPLAINER (Pseudo philosophicus pedantus)

FISHERMAN (Pescadoris immobilis)

EXPLAINER (Pseudo philosophicus pedantus)

Tracks: Locomotion distinguished by frequent pauses for lectures.

Appearance: Carries sufficient field guides, pamphlets, and maps to be mistaken for a park service literature stand.

Call: "It's not a chipmunk, it's a golden mantled ground squirrel."

Where found: Interpretive nature trails—usually noting errors in displays.

Feeding habits: A scientifically designed well balanced diet.

Scat: Inaccurate brochures.

FISHERMAN (Pescadoris immobilis)

Tracks: Wader tracks surrounded by scuff marks from dangling gear.

Appearance: Wears vest with hundreds of pockets all stuffed with strange pieces of metal and plastic.

Call: "What are you using?"

Where found: Rivers, lakes

Feeding habits: Beer. Fish when available, otherwise may nibble spare nightcrawlers

Scat: Fly tying gear, line.

GEARHEAD (Technocratus obsessivus)

GORPER/GORPHEAD/GRANOLAHEAD

GEARHEAD (Technocratus obsessivus)

Tracks: Only crampon marks to be found on
   paved trails.

Appearance: Carries 3000 cubic cm backpack,
   mountaineering boots , ice axe, and camera,
   on 1 mile desert nature trail.

Call: "I think I need to upgrade to a newer
   model."

Where found: As far from the trailhead as he can
   carry his gear—usually under 500 feet.

Feeding habits: Chicken tetrachloride and similar
   dehydrated substances.

Scat: Enough repair materials to stock a retail
   store.

GORPER/GORPHEAD/GRANOLAHEAD
(Homo organicus)

Tracks: Earth shoe impressions.

Appearance: The females of the species have stringy dirty
   blonde hair worn in a bun, and wear calf length print
   skirts, Greenpeace T-shirts, rag wool socks, and hiking
   boots. Males have scrawny beards, wear jeans, peace T-
   shirts, wools socks, and sandals. Both genders wear
   granny glasses and carry army surplus day packs.

Call: "It's holistic."

Where found: Any place where they can get back to nature.

Feeding habits: They eat a mixture of tofu, sprouts,
   and sunflower seeds with miso dressing.

Scat: Granolaheads never drop anything on the trails
   and will often collect refuse left by other species.

KRAUT (Dammen germanicæ)

LOCAL (Rubis localis)

KRAUT (Dammen germanicæ)

Tracks: Sensible pumps.

Appearance: Wears sensible trousers and man-tailored
  shirt in neutral colors. Always carries large (2 gallon
  capacity) shoulderbag. Generally maintains steady
  deliberate pace on trails, but when startled can move
  surprisingly fast for creature of its considerable bulk.
  Female of species generally more common than male.

Call: Guten tag.

Where found: Originally confined to the Black Forest
  and the Alps, has spread across the globe. May
  appear up to 20 miles from backcountry trailheads.

Feeding habits: Subsists primarily on black bread,
  sausages, and strong smelling cheeses.

Scat: Usually very neat but occasionally overlooks
  small crumbs of food.

LOCAL (Rubis localis)

Tracks: Usually rides ATV. Feet only touch ground
  when changing tires.

Appearance: Sears jeans. Works at area.

Call: "Goddamn tourists."

Where found: Service roads, gas stations.

Feeding habits: Mainly Big Macs, tortilla chips and
  salsa, and doughnuts, but will eat anything—
  including road kills.

Scat: Junk food wrappers.

Miscellaneous: Frequently mistaken for Wafflestomper.
  Two species have been known to crossbreed.

MIDDLE AMERICAN (Winnebagus americanus)

MIDDLE AMERICAN (Winnebagus americanus)

Tracks: Sneakers from large discount chain.

Appearance: Usually wears Bermuda shorts and knit shirts. Carries 35mm point and shoot camera.

Call: "The engine is overheating again."

Where found: Scenic overlooks.

Feeding habits: Believes in do-it-yourself meals to save money. Prime ingredients are Wonder bread, ham, mayo, potato chips, and pop.

Scat: Empty Miracle Whip jars, outdated highway maps, and discount coupons.

MORMON FAMILY (Mormani obesi)

Tracks: Up to twenty sets of identically shaped tracks of varying sizes made by shoes all bought at the same sale.

Appearance: Blonde hair. Bodies covered in soft fabrics in pastel colors.

Call: High pitched piercing cries of "Oh my heck!"

Where found: Common in Utah, accidental in California, Arizona, and Idaho.

Feeding habits: Eats steadily and constantly, favoring ice cream, multi-layer jello salads, and milkshakes.

Scat: Diet seven up bottles; aerosol hairspray cans.

NIPPON (Horde orientalis)

PHOTO NERD (Nerdus camera)

NIPPON (Horde orientalis)

Tracks: Pointed toed shoes.

Appearance: Males dress in dark colored suits, ties, white shirts, and black dress shoes. Females are inconspicuous. The Nippon is a social animal, and rarely appears in groups of less than fifty.

Call: Soft conversation murmurs, frequent clicking of expensive cameras.

Where found: Nippon flocks frequent all major tourist attractions.

Feeding habits: Eats raw fish and seaweed at home, indigenous foods while travelling.

Scat: Meticulously neat.

PHOTO NERD (Nerdus camera)

Tracks: Leaves Bogen tripod impressions every two or three feet.

Appearance: Generally invisible under hood of view camera.

Call: "More interesting visual image"

Where found: 30 feet from scenic overlook— shooting from unusual angle.

Feeding habits: Subsists entirely on T-Max developer fumes.

Scat: Lens caps, filters, and compressed air canisters.

RANGER/RANGERETTE (Bureaucratus officius)

RECALCITRANT WIFE (Femina incompositus)

RANGER/RANGERETTE (Bureaucratus officius)

Tracks: Very precise.

Appearance: Neatly pressed park service uniform.

Call: "Don't get eaten by griz on my shift, please!"

Where found: Inside park headquarters.

Feeding habits: Does not eat while on duty.

Scat: Occasionally loses track of carbons from forms in triplicate.

RECALCITRANT WIFE (Femina incompositus)

Tracks: High heeled sandals.

Appearance: Only person on raft trip wearing high heels, nylons, and dress.

Call: "My feet hurt."

Where found: No further from car than is absolutely necessary. Has been known to spend entire vacation feeding squirrels in parking lots while husband take pictures from scenic overlooks.

Feeding habits: Never eats away from home because the food is so bad and overpriced.

Scat: Empty nail polish bottles.

TRAVEL WRITER (Scribelerius scruffius)

VIDEO MANIAC (Camera dementia)

TRAVEL WRITER (Scribelerius scruffius)

Tracks: Uneven due to mismatched running shoes.

Appearance: When found in city parks, frequently picked up on vagrancy charges due to age and decrepitude of clothing.

Call: "Would you mind signing a model release?"

Where found: Anyplace so entirely remote and unappealing as to have remained "undiscovered".

Feeding habits: Doesn't have time to eat, but ingests substantially quantities of plastic when absentmindedly chewing pens.

Scat: Trail of pens, pencils, lens caps, Fuji 35 mm film containers, and unsigned model releases.

VIDEO MANIAC (Camera dementia)

Tracks: Deep impressions due to weight of camera gear.

Appearance: Slowly panning camera to get 10 minute video of perfectly still rocks.

Call: "Emma, Susie, & Jimmy stand over there so I can get a picture of all of you in front of the scenery. We're in—honey, which national park are we in?"

Where found: Anyplace with good car access.

Feeding habits: Popcorn and soda pop.

Scat: Discharged battery packs.

WAFFLESTOMPER (Beerbellius giganticus)

WAFFLESTOMPER (Beerbellius giganticus)

Tracks: Big prints. May be origin of "Yeti" myths.

Appearance: Large and hiristute. Often dresses as mountain man.

Call: "Goddamn government."

Where found: Anywhere he damn well pleases. That's why he has 4 wheel drive.

Feeding habits: Fights off the turkey vultures for a choice road kill.

Scat: Beer cans crumpled in one hand and tossed from window of pickup truck.

Down By The Riverside

Many of the more attractive or unusual species in America's rivers such as the playful river otter or the exotic squawfish are diminished in numbers or facing extinction, while other, often less desirable inhabitants are flourishing and proliferating. This chapter enables quick and accurate identification of many of the more commonly occurring inhabitants of our country's scenic rivers.

BLM/USFS/NPS RIVER OFFICIAL (Dufus officialis)

BLM/USFS/NPS RIVER OFFICIAL (Dufus officialis)

Tracks: Heels and pointed toes of gleaming dress pumps.

Appearance: Neatly pressed brown and tan uniform.

Call: "May I see your permit, please? The permit looks O.K. Now I need to see one coast guard approved PFD for every member of party, bailer, boat repair kit, first aid kit, one paddle and one spare for every member of party, chemical toilet, throw rope ... Look, I know you're only floating three miles of flat water, but I DIDN'T MAKE THE RULES."

Where Found: Exclusively at landing ramps and visitor offices.

Feeding Habits: Subsists entirely on paperwork and permit waiting lists.

Scat: Discarded carbons from triplicate forms.

BOY SCOUT TROOP (Grummanus obnoxious)

Tracks: Leaves long silver streaks indiscrimanently on rocks, gravel bars, and trees.

Appearance: Large packs of small green clad beings, following larger beings of similar appearance.

Call: Sufficiently large volume of high pitched shrieks, whines, and giggles that no individual sounds are distinguishable.

Where Found: Wrapped around only boulder on 100 mile stretch of calm river.

Feeding Habits: Burnt marshmallows, frozen hot dogs, and singed Wonder bread.

Scat: Pop bottles, trashed pocket knives, hot dog buns, mayonnaise jars, paper towels, torn sleeping bags, spare clothes, spray-on bug repellent canisters, and occasional dismembered Scoutmasters.

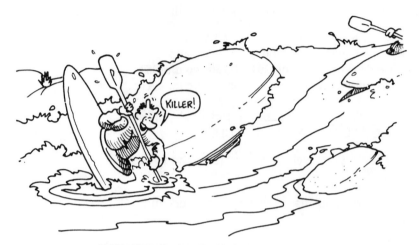

KAYAKER (Imbecilis invertus major)

MARATHON CANOE RACERS (Aerobicus fluvialis kevlar)

KAYAKER (Imbecilis invertus major)

Tracks: Serpentine wake punctuated by occasional moments upsidedown or standing on one end.

Appearance Oddly misshapen head, caused by hitting rocks while floating upside down through rapids.

Call: "Killer!" An all-purpose nasal cry resulting from plugged sinuses.

Where Found: At bottom of deep holes and behind streambed rocks.

Feeding Habits: Ingests large quantities of silt and river water, and an occasional slow moving catfish.

Scat: Leaves small bloody streaks and matted hair on river bottom.

MARATHON CANOE RACERS
(Aerobicus fluvialis kevlar)

Tracks: Tend to move in straight lines, disregarding all obstacles in path, including other boats, logjams, and house sized boulders.

Appearance: Dress in aerodynamic layers to avoid being slowed down by air resistance.

Call: "More efficient."

Where Found: Training.

Feeding Habits: A scientifically designed diet consisting of at least 65% complex carbohydrates, 15% protein, and 20% things picked up at the nearest 7-11 after a tough training session.

Scat: Splinters from thin light weight 14 degree bent shaft paddle used to pry shattered remnants of featherweight canoe off rock.

POWER BOATERS (Propellus petrolealis shreddus)

SQUIRT BOATER (Imbecilis invertus minor)

POWER BOATERS (Propellus petrolealis shreddus)

Tracks: Distinct slick of oil, gas, and/or diesel in association with large V-waves.

Appearance: Wears windbreaker, polo shirt, long pants, and topsiders without socks. Does not expect to get wet.

Call: "Raise the prop!"

Where Found: Stuck on sandbar a few miles from launch ramp.

Feeding Habits: Supplements beer diet with wide variety of insect life caught in teeth while travelling at high speeds.

Scat: Beer cans, oils cans, shredded propellers, muddy shoes and Mastercard receipts. Home ranges easily identifiable by large volumes of scat.

SQUIRT BOATER (Imbecilis invertus minor)

Tracks: Partially to completely submerged, re-surfacing for air at infrequent intervals like a spooked loon.

Appearance: Similar to centaur, except bottom half looks like a Salvador Dali representation of a plastic fork half melted in a campfire.

Call: Usually makes noises similar to spooked loon. Researchers theorize that this may be result of brain damage due to prolonged oxygen deprivation while under water.

Where Found: Deep rivers.

Feeding Habits: Strains algae from river like baleen whale.

Scat: Anything that won't fit in low volume boat including spare clothes, repair kit, and unneeded appendages like little toes and kneecaps.

RIVER BABE (Courtesana aqua) **RIVER SCUM** (Flotsam fluvialis)

RIVER BABE (Courtesana aqua)

Tracks: Small flakes of toenail polish impressed in footprints.

Appearance: Recognizable by blow dried blonde hair, perfect tan, and nail polish. Clothing ranges from minimal to non-existent.

Call: Continuous high pitched squeals when running white water.

Where Found: Bow of tandem canoe or front of raft. Often found in courtship with Raftus opulentus or Flotsam fluvialis.

Feeding Habits: Diet pop, raw veggies, and candy bars.

Scat: Empty makeup containers.

RIVER SCUM (Flotsam fluvialis)

Tracks: Leaves distinct impressions from soles of Teva river sandals everywhere—including waist deep snow.

Appearance: Sun tan acts as camouflage, being precisely the same colour as dried river slime—in fact, it may be river slime. Check for white Teva lines on feet.

Call: "Keep on paddling!"

Where Found: Frequent proximity to river mud banks confirms Aristotelian theory of spontaneous generation of lower life forms from inanimate matter.

Feeding Habits: This scavenger will consume food avoided by turkey vultures.

Scat: Odd pieces of neoprene and duct tape.

WADERS (Piscator neoprenii)

WHITEWATER CANOEIST (Navicularius natator)

WADERS (Piscator neoprenii)

Tracks: Large postholes.

Appearance: Human torso with red baseball cap appears above camouflage rubber.

Call: "Don't snag my line!"

Where Found: Eddies also used by kayakers, canoeists, and rafters. Waders are extremely territorial and will defend foraging grounds aggressively. Females are exceedingly rare.

Feeding Habits: Ample supply of tuna sandwiches, in case no fish are caught.

Scat: Web-like lengths of near invisible line and barbed hooks draped off bushes, snags, and boulders along stream. These invariably interact unfavorably with inflatable boats.

WHITEWATER CANOEIST (Navicularius natator)

Tracks: Paddler's position may be ascertained by location of long trail of bubbles following swamped boat downstream.

Appearance: It is rumored that the average canoeist would look like a human being if you washed off the dried river slime, but no one has dared try to verify this rumor empirically.

Call: "I though I'd tied that in better."

Where Found: Under large clouds of mosquitoes in remote Northern rivers.

Feeding Habits: Inadvertently rehydrated food from improperly sealed dry bags.

Scat: Streaks of red or green gel coat on numerous boulders.

INNER TUBERS (Bolgnas indolentus)

INNER TUBERS (Bolgnas indolentus)

Tracks: Wide slug like trails where tube has been dragged from car to river.

Appearance: Wear baggy shorts, T-shirts, thong sandals, and 2 day growth of beard (both males and females).

Call: "That was fun! Let's do it again."

Where Found: Rapids with good road access. Tubers have been know to require hospitalization when removed further than 200 yards from nearest beer cooler.

Feeding Habits: Food buyable at drive through windows—no respectable store will allow them inside.

Scat: Blown out sandals, lost hats, punctured tubes.

COMMERCIAL RAFT (Raftus opulentus)

Tracks: Path through biggest waves of rapids, interspersed with inadvertent eddy turns and wall slams.

Appearance: One moderately competent oarsman perched behind fifteen shrieking adolescents (ranging in chronological age from 12 - 55) in identical orange PFDs.

Call: "Water fight!"

Where Found : Have overbred in some riparian habitats to near elimination of all competing species due to symbiotic relationship with Dufus Officialis.

Feeding Habits: Luxurious meals from giant coolers, including hamburgers, chips, raw veggies, sandwiches, fruit, chilled pop, and cookies.

Scat: Paper and human waste scattered by the 36 people unwilling to line up for the 2 chemical toilets.

RENTED RAFTERS (Raftus vilis)

SHUTTLE DRIVER (Caravanus hazardous locali)

RENTED RAFTERS (Raftus vilis)

Tracks: Float in current like piece of driftwood.

Appearance: Shows no sign of apparent life until slams into hole or wall, unceremoniously dumping all occupants into river, at which point demonstrates organization similar to disturbed anthill.

Call: "I think I hear something ahead. Pass me another beer, willya?"

Where Found: Regrouping on shore after flips.

Feeding Habits: Occasionally confuses sun tan lotion with mayo, resulting in unusual flavoring of sandwiches, which passes unnoticed due to general strangeness of recipes and degree of intoxication of diners.

Scat: Beer cans, government brochures, forgotten crew members, ammo boxes with such inessentials as patch kit and first aid gear left on beaches.

SHUTTLE DRIVER (Caravanus hazardous locali)

Tracks: Can back van with raft trailer down narrow jeep road at 30 degree incline without jack-knifing. Often attempts to reproduce this feat on crowded freeways at rush hour, much to the dismay of fellow motorists.

Appearance: Darkly tanned left arm contrasts strongly with pale body.

Call: "Am I O.K. on the right?"

Where Found: Underneath decrepit van 20 miles from highway, wrench in hand.

Feeding Habits: Eats whatever the paying customers do not consume, resulting in such things as sandwiches consisting of two pickles, a tomato slice, half an onion, and three oreos, on rye toast.

Scat: Oil trails from hammered vans driven on "high clearance vehicles only" roads.

At The Campgrounds

Campgrounds provide many excellent opportunities to watch humans in the outdoors before they bed down for the night. Many competing species frequent these areas and territorial battles are common.

BANDY-LEGGED GEEK (Ornithologus trivialis)

BASIC STONED CAMPER (Campus cannabis)

BANDY-LEGGED GEEK (Ornithologus trivialis)

Tracks: Carefully eradicates all tracks leading to blind.

Appearance: Only visible indication of its presence is the appearance of binoculars or camera lens protruding from blind.

Call: "I added three to my life list today."

Where Found: Anywhere birds congregate.

Feeding Habits: Nibbles bird seed and spare pieces of camouflage tape.

Scat: Loose pages from well-thumbed field guides.

BASIC STONED CAMPER (Campus cannabis)

Tracks: Generally torpor occasionally punctuated by solo dances in a rhythm nearly corresponding to the sounds of the Grateful Dead from the battery powered boom box.

Appearance: Eyebrows and hair which haven't quite recovered from overly enthusiastic priming of an optimus cookstove.

Call: "Mellow out, dude."

Where Found: Colorado and neighboring states.

Feeding Habits: Munchies

Scat: Roaches, tortilla chips, cassettes of sixties rock.

CAMPGROUND HOSTS (Winnebagus hospitalus)

HUNTING PARTY (Huntus inselectivus)

CAMPGROUND HOSTS (Winnebagus hospitalus)

Tracks: Follow regular trail around campground.

Appearance: Recognizable by grey hair, comfortable clothes, and permanent smile.

Call: "You poor things. You look like you haven't had a decent meal in weeks."

Where Found: In centrally located RV site, feeding hundreds of hardy self sufficient campers who swear never to say anything nasty about RVs ever again.

Feeding Habits: Remains of wholesome hot meals that they prepare for others.

Scat: Leave out food for wild animals.

HUNTING PARTY (Huntus inselectivus)

Tracks: Huge mounds of dirt excavated by 4x4 trying to traverse impassable logging road.

Appearance: Fully covered by camouflage gear including face and hands, over which they wear bright orange blaze so they will be easily visible.

Call: Up to fifteen hour long revoltingly precise stories about things they've killed.

Where Found: Never more than 100 yards from pickup truck.

Feeding Habits: Eat anything they shoot including squirrels, skunks, raccoons, and coyotes.

Scat: Cartridge cases, miscellaneous moving objects (bushes, ATVs, horses, or other hunters) mistaken for legitimate pray.

MID-LIFE MALE (Testosteronous excessivus)

ROCK CLIMBERS (Odoratus verticalis)

MID-LIFE MALE (Testosteronous excessivus)

Tracks: Irregular due to blister from new hiking boots.

Appearance: Cropped T-shirt, and bike shorts to show off weight-lifting muscles, new hiking books, and tanning booth tan.

Call: "Hey, babe, need someone to help you set up that tent?"

Where Found: Curled up in Corvette, because newly discovered toughness isn't quite up to bugs and things that make noises in the night.

Feeding Habits: Gourmet take-out from cooler.

Scat: Cigarette butts, Molson Ale bottles.

ROCK CLIMBERS (Odoratus verticalis)

Tracks: Scuff marks from Tevas used for approach hikes. They only wear their shoes on the rock.

Appearance: Completely covered with rock dust, chalk, and dirt. Cuts on fingers patched with superglue so they'll be able to climb the next morning.

Call: "Rope!"

Where Found: In porta-ledges attached to convenient trees. Serious climbers sleep better dangling in mid-air even in RV parks.

Feeding habits: Subsist mainly on ERG and candy bars

Scat: Chopped bolts, webbing, awkwardly placed pro.

FAMILY OUTING (Swarm familias)

Tracks: Churned areas that look like parts of San Francisco after an earthquake.

Appearance: Large heterogeneous flock ranging from one foot tall to over six feet in six inch increments. Usually includes screaming baby, lost toddler, two kids having mud fight, exquisitely made-up female teenager, male adolescent with weird hair in rock band T-shirt, and two or more sunburned adults.

Call: "If you do that once more, we'll just pack up and head straight back home."

Where Found: Inexpensive and easily accessible car camping.

Feeding Habits: Eats bologna, lettuce, and tomato sandwiches on white bread with Miracle Whip, except for the Johnny, who won't eat anything green, and Billy, who won't eat bread crusts, and Susie who eats only vegetables because she's on a diet, and Mother, who's too busy feeding the baby to eat anything at all.

Scat: Disposable diapers, Miracle Whip jars.

On The Lakes

The shores and waters of North American lakes are inhabited by a variety of creatures—some human, some inhuman, and some hybrid. The majority of these creatures are harmless, but it is best to avoid the more strongly territorial species.

CANOEING COUPLE (Canoe tandemus flailus)

COMMON FISHERMAN (Piscator localis vulgaris)

Tracks: Heavily eroded trail formed by years of repeated use.

Appearance: Wears his fishing clothes—because his wife won't allow him out with his boat in his work clothes.

Call: "I remember twenty years ago, before ... "

Where Found : Same place, every sunny Sunday each summer for thirty years except for the week he's out of town on a big fishing trip with his buddies.

Feeding Habits: Nibbles on spare bait—including cheese, marshmallows, and mealworms.

Scat: Anything he forgets, he'll pick up next week.

CANOEING COUPLE (Canoe tandemus flailus)

Tracks: Follows erratic course as paddlers switch sides at random intervals.

Appearance: Husband sits in stern and yells instructions at hysterical wife in bow.

Call: "Paddle harder. No. On the other side. And hold your paddle like I showed you. No. Not like that. Just do what I tell you. And faster. ... ARE YOU DEAF?"

Where Found: Flailing in the center of a windy lake.

Feeding Habits: Husband is too busy paddling and yelling instruction to eat; wife consumes substantial quantities of polish while chewing finger nails.

Scat: PFD that husband didn't need because he won a canoeing merit badge thirty years ago at scout camp.

JET SKIER (Donor organus)

FLYFISHERMAN (Piscator nobilis)

Tracks: Footprints followed by long thin scratches from trailing gear.

Appearance: Thousands of vest pockets stuffed with mysterious bits of gear, including feathers, plastic lures, hooks, line, and a few toy plastic Teenage Mutant Ninja Turtles which his wife thought might be part of his fishing tackle.

Call: "It's my own variation on a yellow caddis ... "

Where Found: Distant rivers and inaccessible streams.

Feeding Habits: Occasionally confuses tackle box with lunch box and constructs lures from oreo cookies while nibbling rooster feathers.

Scat: Small feathers and bright plastic objects from fly box.

JET SKIER (Donor organus)

Tracks: Convoluted wake terminated by long line of bubbles and fuel where the motor died.

Appearance: Wears red or yellow baseball cap with bill turned backwards, PFD, and jams.

Call: "Watch this!"

Where Found: Floating in middle of lake repairing broken motor.

Feeding Habits: Enjoys complex cocktails of Muscatel, Everclear, and grape juice, but will settle for Coor's Light.

Scat: Pieces of motor left over after it's been fixed.

LOCAL MOTOR BOATER
(Navicularis rubus machina)

LOCAL MOTOR BOATER
(Navicularis rubus machina)

Tracks: Large clouds of black smoke emitted by badly
maintained motor.

Appearance: Wears olive green Sears work pants,
checked flannel shirt, and Caterpillar baseball cap
liberally coated with grease and motor oil.

Call: "That's three of gas, and one of oil—or was that
a quart or a pint we put in last time?"

Where Found: Small town reservoirs.

Feeding Habits: Eats whatever the wife packs in the
lunch box.

Scat: Plastic pint size motor-oil containers.

SCULLERS (Navicularis aerobicus extremis)

Tracks: Long narrow wake abruptly terminated by
obstacle unnoticed due to backward locomotion.

Appearance: Shoulders at least twice the width of
rowing shell.

Call: Rhythmical grunts in time with with motion of
oars.

Where Found: Urban lakes and rivers.

Feeding Habits: Protein powder, amino acids, and
steroids.

Scat: Samples that failed urine tests.

SOLO FREE STYLE CANOEIST
(Navicularis choreogos)

SOLO FREE STYLE CANOEIST
(Navicularis choreogos)

Tracks: Making 180 pivot in center of pond without any forward motion—which is fortunate because pond is only six feet longer than canoe.

Appearance: Permanently tilted towards paddling side as a result of hours spent balancing canoe on one rail and low brace.

Call: Profound silence so as not to disturb concentration.

Where Found: Ponds so small that not even the most miniscule waves can form to disrupt exquisite maneuvers.

Feeding Habits: Never found more than half hour drive from restaurant.

Scat: Paddle covers and unused PFD.

SPEED BOATER (Navicularis hyperactivis)

Tracks: Large circles around all available bodies of water, often pursued by Officialis publicus.

Appearance: Young. This phase rarely persists beyond adolescence (ages 18 - 45 for males).

Call: Any calls are completely overwhelmed by loud buzz of motor.

Where Found: Is constantly in motion unless severely injured.

Feeding Habits: Subsists entirely on adrenaline and excess testosterone.

Scat: Shattered fiberglass covering up to one mile radius after collisions with other boats or immovable objects.

WATER SKIER (Gorilla aqua)

WATER SKIER (Gorilla aqua)

Tracks: Elegant slalom patterns across wake of tow
  boat.

Appearance: Immediate recognizable by elongated
  arms from being dragged several miles face down
  behind motor boat after falling.

Call: "Turn!"

Where Found: In center of whirlpool as tow boat
  circles around to pick them up.

Feeding Habits: Leaves tooth marks on tow bars
  when arms alone aren't strong enough to hold on.

Scat: Dropped second skis.

WINDSURFER (Detritus zephyrus)

Tracks: Dramatic plume of water arcs behind board
  terminated by a large splash when the windsurfer
  misjudges a wave.

Appearance: Windblown.

Call: "Nuclear!"

Where Found: Drifting in middle of lake waiting for
  wind to pick up again.

Feeding Habits: Only eats on totally calm days.

Scat: Biners and webbing from badly adjusted
  harness.

WORM DROWNER (Piscator clueless)

WORM DROWNER (Piscator clueless)

Tracks: Wanders aimlessly in circles looking for a
good stretch of shoreline on which to set up his
lawn chairs.

Appearance: Frustrated because he doesn't
understand why everyone else is catching so many
more fish than he is.

Call: "I didn't know that I needed a license."

Where Found: Easily accessible bodies of water.

Feeding Habits: Eats whatever he catches, including
carp, catfish, and old truck tires.

Scat: Broken $9.99 K-Mart fishing rod that didn't
catch anything.

FLOATING PARTY (Studentus inebrius)

Tracks: Erratic travel due to helmsman having right
arm around girlfriend, can of beer in left hand, and
steering with knee.

Appearance: Rented boat overflowing with young
hard bodies, beer coolers, bags of pretzels, boom
box, cassette tapes, and discarded items of
clothing.

Call: "Let's party!"

Where Found: Congregate at this year's trendy
destination during Spring break and other school
holidays.

Feeding Habits: Will eat anything of which their
mothers might disapprove. Sometimes manage
balanced diet of pizza, beer, pretzels, and Snickers
bars.

Scat: Extraneous pieces of feminine apparel.

KIDS IN INFLATABLES (Innocens perditus)

Tracks: Large splashes from waterfights.

Appearance: Small bodies completely concealed by oversized PFDs and flailing paddles. Permanently dripping noses and piercing cries have led researchers to speculate on possible deliberate abandonment by parents.

Call: "Help!"

Where Found: Disappearing over horizon.

Feeding Habits: Have been observed to steal bread from ducks.

Scat: Kid brother tossed overboard for unforgivable sin of eating something recently removed from left nostril.

LIVERY TURKEY (Meleagris gallopavo rentus)

Tracks: Leaves long silver streaks on every rock within 100 yards of anything that looks like a landing area.

Appearance: Wears new jeans, hiking boots, red flannel shirt, and poncho.

Call: "How did he say we were supposed to steer this thing?"

Where Found: Boundary Waters Canoe Area.

Feeding Habits: Steaks and beer until the ice in the cooler melts, then peanut butter sandwiches.

Scat: Beer cans, plastic wrappers, fishing line, lures, and spare paddle partially burnt for firewood.

DAY SAILOR (Felis hobius)

Tracks: Blown in tight circles around center of lake due to rudder being jammed in fixed position.

Appearance: Wears all white polo shirts and pants and brown topsiders without socks.

Call: "No. Not THAT line."

Where Found: Becalmed.

Feeding Habits: Chews for hours on knots that won't come untied.

Scat: Hopelessly tangled lines and shredded sails.

FISH/GAME/WILDLIFE WARDEN (Officialis publicus)

Tracks: Large ruts from government issue GMC pickup truck.

Appearance: Left arm matches tan colour of pickup truck; rest of body is concealed by cab and uniform.

Call: "I need to see your license."

Where Found: Where not wanted.

Feeding Habits: Nibbles ends of spare pens and pencils while waiting for fishermen to produce lost license.

Scat: Citations nearly issued to relatives of prominent local politicians.

In Snow; Real or Artificial

The inhabitants of snow country tend to be fast moving, bright, and colorful with a variety of idiosyncratic habits well worth observing—so long as you remember to stay off the trails while stopping to watch.

ANKLEBITER (Snowboardus horribilis minor)

ANKLEBITER (Snowboardus horribilis minor)

Tracks: Invisible between the moguls.

Appearance: Generally looks like a smaller and dirtier
version of its parents.

Call: "I'm hungry."

Where Found: Underfoot.

Feeding Habits: Omnivorous. Known to steal bread
from pigeons.

Scat: Miscellaneous small pieces of brightly colored
plastic.

CLINIC JUNKIE (Scholia obsessivus)

Tracks: Precisely imitate those of instructor.

Appearance: So covered with NASTAR and clinic pins
that cloth of parka is completely obscured.

Call: "Do I need to use more knee angulation in my
A-frame?"

Where Found: Resorts with PSIA approved ski schools
only.

Feeding Habits: Diet scientifically designed by clinic
nutritionist.

Scat: Mimeographed handouts.

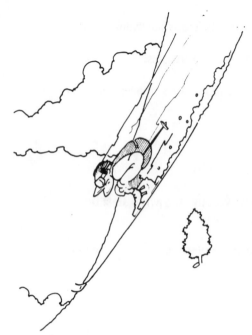

DOWNHILL RACER (Declivus implacabilis)

GOSSIPING FEMALES (Femina immobilia socialia)

DOWNHILL RACER (Declivus implacabilis)

Tracks: Figure elevens down steepest bowls at resort.

Appearance: An aerodymanic blur moving at uniformly high speed on 223 cm. skis.

Call: "Left!"

Where Found: Steeps and good cruising runs.

Feeding Habits: Eats scientifically designed energy bars on lifts. Occasionally ingests hot wax or P-tex by accident.

Scat: Liquid wax, pocket stone, and duct tape.

GOSSIPING FEMALES (Femina immobilia socialia)

Tracks: Due to general immobility, they rarely leave tracks.

Appearance: Resemble clothing advertisements in skiing magazine from a distance. On close observation, these women average 20 years older and 30% heavier than most ski models.

Call: "We didn't know we were blocking the trail."

Where Found: Standing still in the center of busy trail.

Feeding Habits: Enjoy long lunches at gourmet resort restaurants.

Scat: Lipstick, mirrors, and jewellery.

PETRIFIED NOVICE (Novitius consternatus)

KNOWLEDGEABLE LOCAL (Eruditus localis)

Tracks: Always follows most direct route to untracked snow.

Appearance: Vintage gear patched with duct tape. Wears garbage bags over army surplus jacket on powder days.

Call: "We really need more snow this year."

Where Found: Never found by tourists except on lifts. Highly secretive to preserve hidden stashes of untracked snow.

Feeding Habits: Never eats resort food.

Scat: Occasionally leaves streaks of P-tex on rock that "wasn't there last year".

PETRIFIED NOVICE (Novitius consternatus)

Tracks: Erratic wedge shaped gouges in snow from partially mastered snowplow.

Appearance: Wears parka, jeans, and wool gloves. Skis are flat on surface of snow, pointing downhill in uneven wedge, while body is twisted to face uphill.

Call: "This is supposed to be fun?"

Where Found: Almost anywhere—due to congenital inability to read trail maps.

Feeding Habits: These are the only skiers naive enough to attempt the $4.95 chili burger/soft drink special at the mid-mountain restaurant.

Scat: Resort brochures, poles, gloves, and hats.

POWDER HOUND (Canis nivea)

Tracks: Perfect S-shaped curves.

Appearance: Gortex shell liberally sprinkled with
snow.

Call: "Don't trash my tracks!"

Where Found: Out of bounds.

Feeding Habits: Inhales large quantities of snow,
supplemented by pine needles when tree skiing.

Scat: Pieps, shovels, and powder cords.

PUNK TEENAGER/SHREDHEAD
(Snowboardus horribilis major)

Tracks: Intricate paths inside half pipe interspersed
with glove prints.

Appearance: Wears only black, lime green, fuschia,
yellow, and orange. Courtship dances involve males
posturing elaborately under chairlifts.

Call: Aggro!

Where Found: Ski resorts during spring break.

Feeding Habits: Beer and free happy hour hors
d'ouevres. Can subsist exclusively on popcorn,
pretzels, and nachos for periods up to 6 months.

Scat: Previous girlfriends.

SUN BATHERS (Courtesana solaris)

Tracks: Phototrophic. Rotates to expose maximum surface area to sun at all times.

Appearance: Darkly and evenly tanned. Precancerous. Will sit shirtless in sub-zero weather if sun appears.

Call: "Would you mind moving? You're blocking my sun"

Where Found: Lawn chairs outside mid-mountain restaurant.

Feeding Habits: Rarely eats.

Scat: Empty bottles of tanning oil, aerosol hair spray containers, reflectors.

TELEMARKER (Free heelus organicus)

Tracks: Long radius S-curves punctuated by 50 yard long stretches thrashed by monumental eggbeaters.

Appearance: Wears red or green Gortex shell, knickers, gaiters, wool cap, leather boots, and backpack.

Call: Notoriously uncommunicative.

Where Found: Back country.

Feeding Habits: Eat granola, gorp, and peanut butter.

Scat: Occasionally shares gorp with small rodents.

YETI (Projectilis oblivious terriblis)

Tracks: Straight tracks running for approximately twenty yards terminating in large crater.

Appearance: Wears discount store insulated parka/bib matching set and short rented skis.

Call: "Watch out! I can't stop!"

Where Found: Beginner slopes unless totally lost.

Feeding Habits: Brought sandwich to save money but discovered that after the fiftieth wipeout of the day, a tuna salad sandwich stored in a pocket becomes an inedible gelatinous mass.

Scat: Ski school brochures advertising unneeded lessons.